I Think of Our Lives

Books by Richard Fein

POETRY

Selected Poems of Yankev Glatshteyn (translations)
Kafka's Ear
At the Turkish Bath
To Move into the House
Ice Like Morsels

PROSE

Robert Lowell
The Dance of Leah

I THINK OF OUR LIVES

New and Selected Poems

Richard Fein

A Donald S. Ellis Book

CREATIVE ARTS BOOK COMPANY
Berkeley • California

I Think of Our Lives is published by Donald S. Ellis and distributed by Creative Arts Book Company.

For information contact:
Creative Arts Book Company
833 Bancroft Way
Berkeley, California 94710

For ordering information call:
1-800-848-7789
Fax: 1-510-848-4844

Acknowledgments

Some of the poems have been slightly revised since their publication in previous books.

Acknowledgment is made to the editors of the following journals in which some of the new poems originally appeared:

European Judaism: "For Three Killed By Stalin"
The Poetry Porch: "Downward"
Shirim: "Saul at En-Dor," "The Third Elder," "Gather me..."
The Southern Review: "To Walt Whitman"

Cover painting, "Cecil Court, London WC 2 (The Refugees)" © R. B. Kitaj, and reproduced with the permission of the Tate Gallery.

ISBN 0-88739-405-1
Library of Congress Catalog Number 2001095287

Printed in the United States of America

For my friend,
George Kalogeris

"There are more important things than childhood. And perhaps I have the prospect of far more childlike happiness, earned by a life of hard work, in my old age than any actual child would have the strength to bear, but which then I shall possess."

Kafka, *Investigations of a Dog*

Contents

Kafka's Ear

At the Turkish Bath

To Move into the House

Ice Like Morsels

New Poems

I

Kafka's Ear

Going to the Store

I

The dank pickle barrel
squat like an ancient cistern.
Mounted in white scum,
pellets of cumin
ringed the staves
inches above the brine.
Aluminum tongs
forked the rim, but
customers dived in by hand,
fishing habits from the old country,
and held a dripping catch,
sensing taste by ruck and hue.
The firm ones seemed cucumbers
with albino tips
and sallow gaps
stroked into the coat of forest green.
Hauled to the surface
their waxy skin glistened,
dripping back to the soup,
suspended hybrids.
The rejects plopped back,
topping the deep shoal
where they settled.
Underneath couched still more,
inert, immersed, patient.
Gathered for ripeness,
they lounged and sopped,
softening, darkening, wrinkling,
loafing into flavor,
soaking—
like my body in the bathtub
in its rubbery, flourishing indolence.

II

I carried home pickles
rubbing in their juice
in an old mayo jar,
a smoky aquarium eased
into the brown paper bag.
My ears perked
for the slosh of seedy brine.
A spreading stain
moistened the bottom of the bag.
Sheltering that blotch in my hand,
working in a finger to pat
and test the dark Manila stain,
I carried home the scent—
catching a whiff of the brine
through glass and paper
and from my own moist palm.

Reading Genesis at Twelve

Lepke, Gurrah, Reles
prowled the badlands of Brownsville
over the border from East Flatbush
where they packed gats,
took corners on two wheels,
riddled rivals for territory,
cut deals to break deals,
sported fawn-colored spats
and swaggered into poolhalls.
They weren't really Jews.
Nowhere in our stores.
Nowhere in my Book of Genesis.

Isaac, Jacob and Joseph
schooled for a profession.
Joseph, the canny New Dealer,
brought us through the Depression,
like Baruch, the rich adviser,
my father's hero, Jewish-American.

Ishmael, Esau and Cain,
Irish or Italian
kids raised on the streets,
were read out of the story,
left to their own devices.
I was steered through Genesis,
a version cut for us.

Visiting My Father's Grave

I dig,
set down my spade
and cradle-in the juniper bush.

> *The worms crawl in,*
> *The worms crawl out,*
> *through the kishkes*
> *and out the mouth.*

But how could they come out of you?
You, under the lid,
snug in the wood.
You, sealed from the dirt,
boxed from the grass.

I never threw myself upon your breast—
never clung so you couldn't unloose me—
never lingered by your side.
You never breathed to me the secret of your longings.

If you came back
and I were still a child
we'd still be apart.

What we lacked
we lacked together.

Making Vocabulary Lists While Learning Yiddish

The letters bundle
down the page—
curling, squarish, stooped, arched,
no capitals,
crooked, paunched, bowed, hooked, rigid,
right-angled, festooned, knotted, flourishing.

I cannot glide over them;
they flag the eye.

װ (*v*ovn)

I wade in these words
slithering in and out of meaning,

אָ (aleph-*or*)

ciphers teasing
or garnering sense,

ר (*r*eysh)

while with English
the prim letters stay in place,
sewn into the word.

Stirred into Yiddish,
steeped in its juices

ט (*t*es)

I soak up its sounds,
and savor *the word!*—

וואָרט (*vort*)

Two *Tkhines*

Tkhina on Leaving Bed After Childbirth

Dear, dear Father—
blessings, thanks—
now that I can leave my bed
and work in the kitchen,
just like all other women.
Guard my feet
that I won't slip
going to the market.
Sad are those who go
without legs
on boards of wheels,
sad the crippled
who hobble on crutches.

Blessings, thanks—
for the blood
that goes from my heart
to my head and my feet;
blessings, thanks—
for the channels
you installed in me
no professor could invent.
Blessings, thanks—
for the pinholes of my nipples,
so my child's throat is not flooded with milk,
for his tiny mouth that finds the nipple,
for his lips that purse and cling,
for the hurt he draws from me.
Dear, gracious God,
keep me from anger and fear

which spoil milk
and keep my child from sucking.
Blessings, thanks—
for my not turning over and smothering him,
for my hand not falling on his mouth,
for allowing me to hear my child cry in the night.

Dear God of this world and the next,
though I only pray in a mother's tongue,
and wait, like Sarah,
for men to return,
send angels' wings to shield my child from the evil eye.
Keep all my sons from heresy.
Guard my daughter from easy ways.
May they live to a hundred and twenty.

Tkhina on Operating a Stall in the Marketplace

Ever-present God,
my heart is as heavy as the buckets
on the shoulders of water carriers,
my mind as dark
as the backs of horses in the marketplace—
more sellers than buyers.
Ever-present God,
I want to be honest,
neither lie nor cheat,
for I know
You see me
huddling near the firepan
by my bin of wrinkled apples.
Every kopeck is dear to me,
my heart claps amazed
how my tongue barks for the sale.

Ever-present God,
help me with Your firm hand,
the same hand that guided Rachel
as she gathered her wares.
Dear, dear god,
the money is little, the pain great.

Ever-present God,
I haven't time for all Your prayers.
Sunset comes
and I should be home for *shabbes.*
The well-to-do Jews are already bathed,
their candles glow in their candlesticks.
By the time I get home
my husband has lit the candles—
that deed You granted women—

but my fingers snuff out the lights.
Then three sins weigh on my conscience—
I am late for *shabbes,*
I curse my husband for lighting the candles,
I pinch them and light them again.
O dear, dear God,
look at what I am—
a woman who ruins *shabbes*
with her quarrels and her curses.

January in Berlin

It gets dark early in Berlin,
by four dusk comes creeping in.
At first a gauzy wane,
whose beige shades lengthen
and thicken to a tawny smear.
Then a dun vapor
begins to curdle and fissure
till a gray grit sweeps the air.
Finally, sallow lights turn
brown streets browner.
By afternoon the trains grow full,
as if everyone knew
it gets dark early in Berlin,
by four dusk comes creeping in.

Walter Benjamin at the Spanish Border

(September 26, 1940)

But for the guard
I would have docked in America
and killed myself there.
Here, I am closer to Paris.

The last of the Europeans,
what would I have done in New York,
an exhibit in the classroom cage
of The New School?
Mourned the library I left behind?
Choked among the bourgeois working class?
Ended up in a story, "The German Refugee"?

I will miss café-caves,
the tilt of Paris streets.
I sauntered my way to clues,
the neon sign
reflected in the asphalt pool.
I will miss the grain of book covers,
films with Adolphe Menjou,
the curses of the German worker.

I would have petered out in New York,
become a prominent stone in Queens.
I didn't have the refugee's pluck.
I looked with the eyes of Lot's wife,
the exile too weak,
or too attached,
to survive.

I took my dose of morphine,
refused a doctor,

turned the book down.

Dead in Port-Bou.
Buried somewhere;
like Moses, God knows where.

To the Memory of a Jewish-American Poet Whose Work Came to Too Little

No phantom cuh'uh'nels trailing scabbards of fungous green,
no fugitive damask gusting across a scorched veranda,
no family plots where skeletons bone up on honor,
no crosses cudgeling creeds of original sin,
no carousing songs for the silver- or blue- or brown-shirts,
no diamond-winged bird beaked in an Indian's breast,
no lunar phases casting the masks of ego—
no, that crank of stage machinery was never yours.

The Great Books weren't hermeneutics for classes
or entitlements of clerisy, but
Everyman editions
fingered from stalls along Fourth Avenue
before you scooted up to Union Square
to catch the fisted Stalinists, wolf
a bite at the Automat, and turn
up Irving Place to see Cocteau or Eisenstein.
You marked up *The Golden Bowl* riding the subway and knew
instinctively where to get off. You
rowed *Walden* in Prospect Park
and coupled on broken springs
in the Havelock Ellis House Plan basement.
You didn't flirt with fascism
to bring forth order and art.
How could you, being Jewish?
It saved you from some idiocies.
Relishing the art of neo-feudalists,
neo-classicists, neo-mythicists,
neo-Confederates, neo-monarchists,
the darlings of *Action Française,*
you never let their *goyishe mishigas*
stop your breathing of their poems.

Though they feared and scorned your origins,
you outsneered them, were your own class enemy—
"The *lumpen-bourgeoisie,*
the counters at the till, the seekers of frigidaires."
You knew the charges of those rightists
without swallowing their cures.
You read them with inward, cherishing ears,
and critical heart.

Yiddish rattled within you
and you had a nose for middle-class fears.
The Depression gave time for Proust,
chess, handball and shooting pool.
Freud gave way to Reich, Lenin to Trotsky.
"The Trotskyists became professors
and the Stalinists went into real estate,"
you summed it up.
Then came your one great poem,
"Elected Father,"
about FDR, that royal democrat
with *pince-nez* and amber cigarette holder
enthroned in his motorized landau at Wheeling
while shaking hands with a coal miner,
who gripped a grimy mess cup in his left hand.
Your poems were steeped
in the brew of history and psyche.

Your Freudian fables
and those brilliant reviews
for *Partisan, Kenyon,* and *Southern*
struck praise from Tate, Wilson and Nabokov.
You reviewed books
like a rightfielder at Ebbets Field
who knew how every fly ball
angled off the scoreboard.

So what went wrong?
Why so few books?
So few poems to last?
You—comedian of table-talk,
master of mimicry, spoof and takeoff:
Lionel Barrymore snarling Lear,
Prufrock pestering in Yiddish,
Mike Quill broguing Yeats at the union hall,
Mussolini balconizing *The Cantos*—
You, the Joyce of the cafeteria spiel.
So what went wrong?

Something kicked loose,
like the time you brought a bag of cherries
to Eliot's reading at the Y
and while he ministered lines
you fingered out the cherries,
munched away,
spat the pits back
and walked out, shaking
the brown bag like a maraca.

So what went wrong?
The orgone box oozed lethal rays—
convections by Perls and Goodman—
the Trotskyites scissored your books—
not a vision left to call your own, except
like a capo you always sat facing the door.
Who knows what evil lurks in the minds of paranoid poets?
Not even the shrink in the shadows can be sure.
Wives betrayed you, friends betrayed you, editors betrayed you, even
"Poetry isn't constant,
you're finally stuck with yourself"—
your last subject
you just suffered
'til you died in a West Side SRO
with the *Daily News* on your chest.

Kafka's Ear

Foliage sprouts beyond your temples.
Rabbits hunker close in your sleep
and munch on your leafy auricles.
I crouch into your crumpled funnel,
sliding down the tube.
I swim in your canals of gloom,
then clamber outwards,
amazed by the coils and grooves.
Each magenta thread,
blurred and wriggling,
is like a Yangtze to me.
You can hear me crinkling
inside your furrowed conch.

At the Turkish Bath

Kafka and Milena in Bed

Asleep like a child,
you slowly and vaguely turn
toward my ribs as I slouch
against the brass bars.
Light seeps into your face.

I tried to ward you off with my diaries
testing you to come closer. I
conspire against myself,
Milena—my faithful translator
coughing up your own blood.
We're no Etruscan couple
laid out at the Hotel Riva.

You murmur for symmetry
during "man's business."
If I kiss the right shoulder
I must kiss the left shoulder.
If I kiss the left nipple.
I must kiss the right nipple.
And so with the eyes, ears and thighs,
elbows, temples and toes.
Then I curl like a Jew at your feet.

I'm so thin
who is there
to make love to?
I will slip into you, Milena,
and disappear.
You will carry me home,
chat with your husband.
You will breathe
and wonder if I'm still there.

Your mouth is open
beside my rib cage.

The Clouds

Land masses on the move, Balkan
cumuli. What was just Denmark...
elongating, warped into Italy.
Faces scallop, or notch and jut.
Mussolini's jaw and forehead
bulk under his ovoid fascist hat.
And then from all the way down here
a cloud can sunder to a flower.
This run of heaven's uncertain, wanton,
even Ovidian—that mottled, deviant
moon squatting in the afternoon sky,
like some homeless buttock.
One cloud, whiter than a sheet
fresh from the washer-dryer,
shades into a pearl-gray tint,
like the handle of Patton's revolver.

At the Turkish Bath

I

His chest, hairy as a gorilla's,
his penis—puckered
under its ruddy dome—
pudgy as a fireplug.
My father and I sat
ass to ass in the steam
with the paunchy, bald men
who sweated a few pounds,
then gnawed on a hot pastrami.

We *shvitzed* away
a Saturday night with his cronies,
their gold capped teeth, hairy nostrils
and throaty Yiddish
foreign to my body—American made.

"My Kaddish," my father introduced me
around the lounges and massage tables.
Naked men were swimming in the pool,
each with his chest of dancing hairs.
They lumbered out and rubbed themselves dry.

II

I still see the pink glow
of the men walking across the marble
floor, their terry cloth
towels knotted at the hip
and stamped in blue,
BESSARABIA BATHS.

"See," my father's skin talked,
"we sit here, sweat it out,
and take a plunge."

Last night
I saw my father
through the frosted shower door.
"We're both naked," he said.
"Let me in."
I stepped closer to the nozzle and drain
and made room for him
in the glistening slabs of the tub.

Prokofiev's "Overture on Hebrew Themes"

(a lyric for Sheva)

Klarnetyidl tsaplt umheymlikh in avir,
Eerie clarinet-Jew quivers in the air,

af der vant ganvet zikh zayn shotn—a ton fun Mem.
his shadow thieves along the wall—a strain of *M.*

Notn un taktn fardreyt er, tener un games.
He despoils notes and measures and scales.

Prokofief hert shpaltungen in ihm.
Prokofiev hears rifts in him.

Geshpante lekn kneytshn zikh, un yomern,
Tense licks pucker, whine,

vi a seksuel vimpernish vos geyt oys un geyt on.
like a sexual whimper dying out, going on.

Nit nur funem fidl, nur fun ale keylim krikht aroys dos yidl.
Jew seeps from all instruments, not just the fiddle.

Zayne klangen nemen iber di luft vos mir otemen,
His sounds invest the air we breathe in,

makhn iber blut vos loyft tsum harts, geyen arop tsu khokhmes .
alter blood driving to the heart, regress to jokes.

In di notn hert Prokofief dos yidl, vu er dringt arayn.
Plaintive, flouting Jew penetrating the notes, Prokofiev hears him.

Yankev Glatshteyn Visits Me in the Coffee Shop

I was facing the back
and didn't see him come in.
He shimmied into the booth
and I knew him right away.
He looked at me, clamped his lips. Sighed.
"I deliberately speak to you
in English because I want you
to understand me perfectly.
Since I died, by the way,
my English is better. I have
long conversations with Marianne Moore
about prose in poetry
and I exchange tales with Yeats—
he's not the snob he used to be.
He tells me a Celtic tale and I
tell him one about Chelm.
It's more literary the life there, but
we don't write anymore.
But that's not what I want to talk about.
It's all good and well you translate me.
You need it more than I do.
I'm in Yiddish for all time.
Not that I mind, mind you.
Be my guest. But you,
you have to translate yourself
into English. Stop fretting
about starting late. Be like Yiddish
literature—grow into your gift.
Don't brood over your unmetrical ear.
Listening to the truth-rattles in you,
your ear will catch on. By the way,
I never mourn Yiddish anymore.
We gather in Peretz's salon-cloud—

our Yiddish will last forever there—
though no one blows in from a shtetl,
manuscript in hand.
Well, *zay gezunt.*"
Absent-mindedly, he unclamped the sugar pourer
from the laminated menu, his fingers
played in the glass fluting; as he
moved out he jarred the table
and my coffee shook.

Of the Jews (1950)

An orthodox rabbi—his father. He,
balletomane, translator of Flaubert,
poetry editor of *Partisan Review,*
signed his pieces, "I. Salmagundi."
Late at night he listened to Schnabel.
Saw "Open City" six times, knew by heart
Pound's Li Po, Lincoln's Second Inaugural,
the batting average of every Dodger.

Muscular as a Cossack riding The Steppes,
his poetry contained the shapes of pity—
a peddler confiding in the ear of his horse.
Ishmael cried, "Call me brother." He felt
himself both at the heart and at the edge.
He compared his work to that jagged "R"
he carved into the binding of *Western Civ*—
his way of saying—"Rabinowitz was here."

In Memory of Rabbi Herman Pollack

After invoking Dolci, Sartre and Sakharov
to condemn the cynicism of Kissinger-Strangelove
and harping on the McCarthy craze that drove
you from Brooklyn College in '53, you unscrewed
the cap, poured the whiskey and wondered
aloud if Sophy entered the elkhound
that trailed you home the day she died.
"'Elky' loves to lie near me when I read.
We ruminate," you said, nursing
the whiskey left in your glass.

Out for bagels and lox next morning, you paused
before a newspaper on the sidewalk and cursed
the house where "that *mamzer* racist
slumlord reads his comics and sports
while gouging rent from his tenants."
Then you bent, laid the paper at his door,
and explained, "He has a bad heart."

The Last Jew in Goshen

That rag-tag multitude
will straggle through the desert,
stumble upon signs,
conjure up a God
who will say,
"I am what you want me to be."
They will scheme new orthodoxies,
ancient practices forgotten.
I'll be the only one in Egypt
who knows why the vests were striped,
why little columns were carved into front doors,
why crescent-shaped letters
glowed between sashbars on the fanlight.
Only I will know the reason the glazed
pitcher sits in the southern window sill,
filled with oil.
I will rest in the pure case of what was,
leaving *them* to an evolving God.
Out of touch they imagine they stay in touch
with quibbling and polemics, exemptions
fostering exemptions, studied connivances,
stories falsifying stories,
profusions of visions.
To them—intoxications around tambourines,
devotions to altars, rods and thrones;
to them—the sybaritic king, sacred crag,
epileptic seer, an ark to lug around.
Mob transformed to a movement, they
will submit to illusions of the desert trek.
Chronicles will appear, imaginings
bridging past and present, minds
clouded with fantasies of choice.
They will smack their lips over new signs, words

rubbed into portents. Revisionists of exile,
they go to one land, end up in another.
But for me...the dominion of what's been,
the songs that abide in the old melodies,
like water that's carved its channel in the stone.
What they have abandoned quickens my blood—
the dwindling jargon frisky in my throat,
idioms poured from old brown bottles
and sweet to my tongue. Stalks of the past
sprout again, I feel them coiling within me.

In Berkeley

(in memory of M.H.T.)

Before I arrived at her apartment I stopped to buy
two bouquets of carnations, one for her, one for Yiddish.
I pressed the button slab on the doorpost. Chimes rang
out, then I heard her shuffling on the other side.
"Vishy, is that you?" she squawked through the door.
After she removed the chain, turned the lock, stood
in the doorway, I reached to shake her hand but she
pecked me on the cheek and drew me in. Her cheeks
were rouged. "The water's almost boiled. Do you like tea?
Help me set the table. Oh, Vishy, I'm so glad you came."
Her shaking hand poured the tea; I kept mine ready to leap.
We stuck our butter knives into the jam, coloring our crackers.
We nibbled, drank our tea, and talked. She supplied me with words,
touched up my pronunciation, waited patiently as I responded.
I concentrated on the vertical furrows above her lips,
the slight mustache, the wetness of her eyes. "What
are you thinking of, tell me, what are you thinking of?"
I hesitated, caught staring, then answered,
"Not what, who. I was thinking of a picture I had seen
of Maud Gonne, when she was quite old, still shining.
You remind me of her, something in the eyes, the pursed lips."
"Oh, Vishy, but I'm a poet, not just an activist." She took
my left hand, her fingers grazing along my palm and then
over my fingers. "You have no choice but to do your work.
One track you ride on is English, one is Yiddish. *Now*, you
must go, the woman is coming to bathe me, unless of course
you want to stay. But your family must be waiting."
Then she bent down and kissed the fingers on my
left hand and kissed the fingers on my right hand.
"These are my kisses for your fingers that type.
Be sure to write and tell me what you're doing. I'll
try to write back, dear Vishy, but write me anyway."
I wrote a few times, sent some poems before she died.
I still see the lines above her lips as she kissed my fingers.

The Old Man in His Apartment

The languor of late Sunday afternoon—
and that vague discontent visits him
as it always has after long lapses,
surrounding him with a longing he can't
explain or name, that seems both outside
and inside him. He wonders why he feels
empty and abandoned yet also
charged by his own vacancy, as if
he's touched some puzzling power of himself.
This longing comes
with that lounging, seeping tawny light—
diffusions of a late Sunday afternoon.
He can feel it come into the room,
drop about him from the window and walls,
and the only words that come to him are
"entrance" and "something else," and he feels
he's a room looking at its furniture.

Broken Pieces

(after Peretz Markish)

Now that my vision's needled inward my eyes
rip open and each one of my nerves sees
my heart has fallen, like a mirror on a stone,
and with a clang it shatters into pieces.

Is it possible that each of the splinters
will testify against me, to the end of my days?
Don't press me—you Old Ideals—don't judge me
till I've recovered every sliver from the breakage.

I try to join them together, piece
by piece. My fingers sparkle and bleed. Yet
no matter how artfully I match the pieces
I only see myself cracked and jagged.

In the midst of my despair, I near a solution, a
black shape—oblique, lean—looms out of my grief.
I see my own shadow behind the mirror, whose silver
pieces are scattered over the field of my life.

To Move into the House

Just After Dawn

I woke to the murmur of my words.
Leaning against the headboard
I yielded to the words
that took me back
to my mother's slow death,
how I finally stopped wishing
I had a sister to take her off my hands,
how we worked through that illness to embrace
and she called me *Ruvn, Ruvn.*
Then I remembered a pushcart
and that day in the wintry '30's
when she chatted with a bearded man in Yiddish
about the old country.
She reached into his pile
of hats and gloves,
pulled out a leathery cap,
fixed it squarely on my head,
looked at me and asked,
"Is it too tight
when you button the flaps?"
They settled on a price.
He put his hand on my head
and I flinched under his blessing.

Manasseh

The old man rocked back and forth, wearing
a little black cap, mumbling a chant, his arms
criss-crossed, his palms flat on our heads.
Father tried to switch the hands, but the old man
wouldn't budge. Now, in tasselled shawl with bands
of black, Ephraim rattles off Hebrew prayers. The old
man gloats.
                        What do I have in common with them?
I have hardly anything in common with myself,
should stand in a corner, content that I can breathe,
away from their blessings, prayers, bobbings and mutterings.

My uncles prowl about, sizing up the place. Stinking
of garlic and saddle bags, they gesticulate, jabber,
trade wisecracks and poke about, running their fingers
along stone doorways, brick walls and painted pots.
Then they check on their camels, wives and kids.
I'll sneak out when nobody's looking, but here's
an uncle now, smiling, a hand towards me, the straps
of his sandals frayed and the leather cracking.
"Hello, Menashe, I'm Uncle Reuben. Come, your uncles
and aunts all want to meet you. Come Menashke. Come."

To the Memory of Irwin Levine

That term we stenciled leaves and whittled
soap sculpture in Mrs. Kendall's art class
I went down into the den of my throat
where I kept droning—
"spinal meningitis...spinal meningitis"—
to ward off your virus.

Yours—the face missing in the graduation picture,
yet year after year you return.
For the first time you speak:
"You bring me back,
but why don't you talk to me,
tell me what's on your mind?"
And now I find myself confiding in you—
talking about mischances, failures, confusions,
how my work stemmed from what I missed,
how my words emerged from what I never faced,
and what I became rose from what
I shunned, feared or spurned. Evasions,
Irwin, filled my bag of tricks.

> We ran our plays on the gravel lot,
> you my blocking back. But someone from
> the opposing line kept breaking through,
> trying to touch me with his two hands.

When the Jewish People Lived in Flatbush

They all gathered at the store—bookies flicking cigarettes,
pimps with golden key chains, dime-a-dozen card sharks,
cops on the take, zoot suiters, and runners for the numbers.
They worked toothpicks between their lips, tilted fedoras
back of the head, spat sunflower shells on the sidewalk.
And everyday standing there among them—*Der Shtumer*—
the dummy. He hauled bundles of papers in from the curb,
swept the sidewalk, stacked soda crates, stared, never spoke.
He didn't walk but heaved and stumbled, a creature
with a shaved head on top of a body that lumbered forward.
While he gaped among the bookies in front of a crepe display,
they liked to drop coins behind his back. He never turned.
Once they made a pot and paid a whore to sleep with him.
The jokes lasted all week. He looked the same, said nothing.
Sherwin Field was caught robbing a clothing store.
Manny Berg did time for fixing a high school game.
Bernie Stern violated the Mann Act.
After I boarded the bus to go to school, I'd look back
at the bunch of them—arguing, spitting, gesturing,
fingering scratch sheets, eyeing girls, lighting up.
There on the sidewalk, in front of the window, or near
the rack of candy and the swirls of the marble counter,
they figured out the odds, laid bets, thumb flicked
a deck or rubbed their palms over clicking dice.

Brooklyn College

To bone up on the French Revolution,
Arlene asked me over.
We opened Tocqueville, went
over ideas, followed our notes
from Professor Bloom's class,
and then she guided my hand
from *L'Ancien Régime* to her breasts.
I yanked her sweater
from her culottes.

After my daughter was born in '61,
I read Professor Bloom had died.
Crossing Broadway, he slipped
in the snow and was hit by a bus.
Holding Marsi in my arms,
I hummed a lullaby, walking around
and around the living room, thinking
of the mind of Solomon Bloom,
once playful, now dead.
I thought of his book
on Marx and the working day,
of the girls he took to bed.
I remembered Arlene, how she
shook off the straps of her bra,
her eyes gazing back at me
as we touched, pupils of desire.

Yiddish

O Yiddish,
I felt your teeth
in my bones.
You cut into my childhood body
like the saw of a bungling magician
that bit through
the woman in the coffin.
Now I comb the stage
of the abandoned theater
for every splinter,
every chip I can lay my hands on.
Where are the bloodstains
that show the clumsy act was here?

It's good to know
you're good for nothing now,
except for the love I show you.
We could never have come together
if you were still teeming on the streets,
re-inventing yourself for textbooks,
commercials, psychotherapy.

You reach for me like a lover wanting
one more kiss.
How long it's taken for us to embrace,
for our tongues to find each other.

Pansies on My Sill

Down toward the star-calyx each magenta petal is stained
with an even darker version of itself. A batik
streak of yellow leaks from the celadon spot at the core.
I reach into the window box and rub a pinch of dirt
between my finger tips. I remember a Sunday morning
when I heard *Bolero* streaming out of a window facing the old
Jewish cemetery in Prague; and then my happiness
on hearing the rhythms repeating, quickening, rising,
gathering to their climax amid the stones and the names.

Photograph of a Jewish Girl in Cracow, 1939

Snow dusts your smart beret,
forehead and hair.
How light your glance, as you stand
in the slush and mud—
button-rims with dark navels,
lapels slanting into the collar,
your bare right hand
sliding into your left sleeve.

If your grandparents had left Cracow,
as mine left Kovno in 1901,
you might have been born in Brooklyn.
We might have gone out together,
necking at the movies,
wondering how far we should go in the dark.

I thought of the powers...

I thought of the powers that visited
Mani Leyb in his last twenty years
when he wrote sonnet after sonnet
and faced his confusions and fears.
In that new stage his themes seized him,
words and rhythms stamping the page,
poems driven by their late powers
as he eyed himself from chin to hair.
Then I thought of how age (before old age)
might drive me down to poetry, down
to that place where I'd meet old sounds
and shapes, where I'd look at myself,
at others, at what I did or hadn't done,
no longer fostering my art of evasion.

In the Caves

Rabid dogs, prowling the rocks, climb toward us,
snort, poke, climb again. They smell us trapped
in the caves. Their ruffs inch forward, their necks
turn. Their tongues coat the air. Saliva strings
from their mouths. They prick their ears and mutter.
They yawn, bored and expectant. They command the ledges,
stand in twos and threes. They are the mountains now.
They are waiting for us to come out to them.

The Procedure

In a hospital gown I climb onto the gurney. The cradle
bars hitched up, an orderly fastens my bracelet I.D.,
the purplish letters of my name blurred at the edges,
like a bad carbon copy. They roll me away, under
the ceiling tiles as perforated as a punchboard.
Two nurses greet me in a small room, each with
a crisp nametag and a badge pinned above a breast.
One asks, "Have a good prep? All cleaned out? "
"Uh-huh," I nod. "Good, good," she chimes, moving
me onto the table. She parts my gown at the buttocks
when the doctor arrives. "Hello. Are we ready?" I can
feel their hands on me now. They're inside me now.
My colon on the monitor looks like a string of pink
poppit beads. First time a man can look up his ass,
I want to say. But better not. They may not like it.
"When the going gets tough, the tough get going,"
the doctor jokes, adding, "Nixon's Attorney General."
"Mitchell," I say, "John Mitchell." "That's right,"
he says. "That's who it was." More air gets pumped in.
The cramps get worse. Hands knead my stomach. "I'm sorry
it hurts," the doctor says. "We have to go all the way
to the cecum." I hurt. I want them to say, "Well,
we've looked inside you and found nothing." But
he's still inside me, a nurse at his side. Finally,
I hear him say, "We're coming out now," and I can
sense their slow retreat as if inch by inch my insides
are left to themselves. The scope slides out of me,
my anus contracts to itself. The doctor announces,
"Well, we're out now," but their air is still inside
of me. A nurse rearranges my gown and all I do is fart.
"Good, good," she encourages. "Let it all out.
It helps the cramps." I fart and fart. "Good."
Are they only their training? They wheel me back, say

"Rest," as if I've been a good but overactive boy.
At home I wake to find my pajamas stained.
I want to fart but shit in my underwear instead.
I remember how I brought my ear to my father's lips
at the end of his days in the nursing home, and he
whispered, as if his words were for my ear alone,
"My body won't listen anymore. I've lost control."

Kafka Moves to Palestine (1925)

(for Allen Tobias)

Like a figurehead on a prow, Dora stood up and leaned
forward in the open car. She spread the skirt
of her coat and shielded me from the wind and the rain
all the way from the sanatorium to the clinic in Vienna.
"Let's leave Europe," I said, "try to change
our lives. Tel Aviv is just the place—
the sun, the sea, that coast, and all those newly
laid out streets...as soon as I'm better we'll set sail."

Here in Palestine I go over the specials of the day.
In my white shirt, bow tie, black jacket and pants
I'm the best and only waiter at Franz and Dora's Konditorei.
I can carry four plates at once—
two in hand, one balanced on the pulse, one
in the crook of the arm. I've learned the knack
of pouring water while moving the pitcher down to
and then high above the glass. I serve the bread.

At night Dora and I still have fun fingering shadow
figures on the wall. We give each silhouette a name,
and they talk to one another, as if they're more
than dark and fidgety shapes. My head in her lap, Dora
reads to me Genesis, Ruth, The Song of Songs.
When I miss something she leans over and translates;
I feel in her face, in her body, all that the words mean.
Then we go over the passage again. In bed she presses
my body to hers, switches from German, "Come, I'll show you
how to make love in Hebrew since you've entered the Holy Land."

Ice Like Morsels

Between Five and Six at the River

The world is buoyant, October air
keen and tinged with saffron. A blessedness
seeps from the day—my eyes avid
as mouths. Diagonal panels of light
lacquer water. The concrete
underarch of the low stone bridge shines,
enigmatic as a crypt that receives the sun.
I can't understand how the light glows
in that undercurve. How could it shine down there?
Then I see how the light angles off those planes
and turns that vault of stone into gold
and rose. I turn to walk on the bridge, gently arched
above that oblique light in the undercroft.

Children, Always Dying

(after Arn Tseytlin)

Children vanish.

Adults—specters
of dead children.

Children, always dying—
even the ones still playing
in the schoolyard, on the stoop,
back of the store, behind the sofa,
in the corner of the bedroom.
Their games are brief—
in a flash they're over.
Adults admonish:
"Don't get dirty."
"Hurry up, we're going."

Children—inventors. Tricksters.
Here one minute, gone the next.

B'klyn

The sauerkraut juice vaporized a bit near the black grill
while the late rays of a winter's day seeped through
the steam on the window and settled on the frankfurters
keeping warm in the bubbly puddle of their own grease.
The teeth of the slicing machine were raised while the hot
pastrami sweated in the metal steamer box. Sam sat
in the back of the store, harnessed in his soiled apron,
wearing a light, white garrison cap, a thin green line
running the rim of the gauzy crater. He was doling out mustard
into waxed paper cones he pinched at the bottom and tucked
in at the top, more enclosed than a roll of pennies. One lonely
customer nursed a glass of tea on an ox-blood formica table
while reading a Yiddish newspaper. I couldn't understand what
he was reading, or even how, his glasses perched on his forehead
as if he had a second set of eyes. The slugs of headlines
fractured and flew off the page—dots, hooks, flecks and squiggles,
severed remnants of letters; black scraps, dispersed, isolated.
Down the page those strokes did the opposite, clung to the letters,
to the serried words, dense, impenetrable, stuck in their
tribal compact of pitch, plaint, age and innuendo. Intruder—
I brooded—what are you doing here, here where I belong,
here where salamis shine in their tight condom wrap of cellophane?
He didn't see me at all, deep in his reading. His tea bag
had bled its last flavor and tone in the tepid water.
I turned my back on him and relished the meats in the glass show-
case,
but I saw him again in the mirror as I stared past my own face.
Hunched over his paper, his body was creased into its folds.
The tea sat a little above the thumb-size indentations
running around the lower third of the glass, grip mold turned
design. His right index finger kept rubbing the same spot
along the saw-toothed edge of the page, the seat of his spoon
couched in the stain it made on the napkin.

My Father's Shoe Store

One day, after my father had died,
I read a poem by Yeats, the one
in which he scorns all those who
"fumble in a greasy till," and I
squirmed. I remembered my father
sitting on a stool and bending
toward his customers' stocking feet,
then rising to become commodore
of the burnt sienna register
that pouted digits lipped in silver.
He poked the buttons, rabbit-
punched a bar, and the till
slammed out, the orange-brown
thorax rasping, gurgling, tinkling
for cash while the black numbers
on the white flags, tipped
like an FBI badge, shot up
in the glass from somewhere deep
in the innards. The only other time
he looked like a man in command
was when he maneuvered the glass-
knobbed shift elbowing upward
from the floor of his green Studebaker.

With Everything We've Got

(after H. Leyvik)

My friend said to me, "We Yiddish poets
should write our last poem and throw
it into a coffin, then, like pallbearers,
carry it through the Jewish neighborhoods.

We'll wrap our poems in blue cloth,
or maybe cover them in plain white,
like the white pages of our books,
which rot in cellars—food for mice.

Or cover them in red crepe, in memory
of poets sentenced to prisons and gulags
or murdered by the hygienic visions
of a despot, Cain dressed in lederhosen.

Even those who've only written a single line
can carry the pine box in our procession
through the Jewish streets, past stores,
synagogues and apartments, schoolyards, alleys.

The youngest poet will lead us; he'll unscrew
his fountain pen, hurl cap, barrel, clip
and point into the gutter. Then we'll do the same,
from East Broadway to the Williamsburg Bridge.

From the Bridge to Brownsville, to Flatbush,
to Brighton Beach, onto Coney Island, Sea Gate,
and the Atlantic. We'll cast away our last poems,
the water coming in, the water going out.

We'll stand at the edge of the ocean
and look at the waves foaming in anger

or in praise of poets who with their own
hands fling their last gifts into the abyss.

And then what?—Then, we'll take the subway
back to our rooms, unhood our typewriters.
On those round, silvered keys, we'll write
an elegy—and give it everything we've got."

Leyvik

I want to dance naked,
gaze at Bathsheba. I want
to live in the mountains
and valleys of Cezanne's tablecloths,
near oranges, a ginger pot, a vase,
dresser drawers with oval
plated keyholes and concave knobs.
I want to stand before his tables,
altars of fruit.

I peeled my tongue from the iron
bar, drew it back into my mouth,
childhood prank turned to winter's blood.
The Czar's police smashed in my door,
caught me red-handed, seized
my pamphlets and printing press,
threw me into solitary.
I huddled with my hallucinations.
Four years later I slogged through the snows,
ended up here on Essex, pasting epaulettes
for night club doormen, drum majors,
and generalissimos under movie marquees.

Even in New York the Cossacks
whip their horses through my poems.

Yiddish Poets Speak to Me from the Grave

Translate us,
as if you were returning
to your childhood,
as if you'd missed it
and now find it—a gift
age has given you.
Translate us,
as if you'd postponed
your own life,
and just now return to it,
happy to find
that nothing
can keep you from us.

When you go down,
when you visit us,
walk where you feared to go.
We will speak Yiddish,
our words shaking off
the darkness and gathering
around you. We will
be patient.
Only now, Ruvn,
only now,
do you know
how long
we've been waiting
for you,
above and below.

Northeast Corridor

(on the way to my reading)

North of New Haven I woke to see
a dog staring at the train, its sorrel
coat shining at the edge of the woods.
The sun appeared and disappeared
among the branches. I gazed
at the dark, furrowed trunks
receding into the depths of their forest.
Then I saw the sculptured shapes
of six Yiddish poets, massive
and cloaked among the trees, like figures
out of Rodin, and I heard them say,
"Read us. We're still alive.
We give you the power of our voices."

The Scholar Returns to His Sources

Like Lot, I learned to be patient.
Finally, I return to the streets
where I charmed girls with Yiddish
folksongs, visited cabarets, took
the trolley to *The Dybbuk.*

Exile's behind me. Done with the noise
of Zion—someone else's youth—
I'll marry Wanda; later, be buried
in the old Jewish Cemetery, as close
to Peretz and Anski as I can get.

I'll turn to dust here, this city
where I made love in Yiddish
and Polish. What do angels know,
admonishers of looking back?

Orpah

("Then Orpah kissed her mother-in-law and returned to her people."
The Book of Ruth)

The cooking, the clothing, the counting, the scrubbing,
the blessings, the sundowns, the stars, the strings.
You couldn't dream, raise sheep, marry somebody, draw
your pail from a well, or name your child without being
part of a scheme, some order, some promise, some plan,
a grand design. I had to turn the meat over and over
on the fire so the savor would incite the smoke
that pleases the inhaling god. I bathed Fridays. I missed
my own hair. Now I like offering fruits to the green
figurine that sits at my door, that shining malachite
with the dome-head, paunch, his feet folded under him.
It's simpler now, no messengers suddenly showing up
for dinner, and you rush around serving them until
they reveal something you have to do, somewhere
you have to go, some future that will be yours, some land,
some cave, some hill, some wall, some stream, some stone,
if you only gesture over candles, sew a curtain, fast
on a certain day, or sit in a tent with the sacred
hides placed on your lap as you watch the seers shaking
over scrolls, reckoning tribal fates, transposing
letters into numbers, then humming and chanting, clustering
in a ring, their arms on each other's shoulders as they go
round and round, stamping the earth with assurances from God.

Naked Hides

They emerged from tree and bush and forest,
on four legs, on two, some crawling, some hopping.
They were straight tailed and curly tailed
and untailed. With swollen udders, pointed ears,
cloven feet—scales, hair, thick plates, naked hides.
They were mewing, bellowing, screeching, braying;
honking, croaking, squeaking, buzzing.
Now I can't remember what they're called.
Or a name comes out of nowhere, like *marmoset,*
and I think of the game I played as a child,
pin the tail on the animal, only I have no idea
where, or on what, to pin the name.

Yesterday I set out to find that old garden.
Wasn't it on Beverly Road off Utica Avenue?
I thought I knew the way, but I got lost,
or maybe I found it, but it had changed so much
I couldn't recognize it. There was a lot,
like the lot I saw when we first left the garden,
the lot with the diagonal shortcut, twisted
wire in the dust, and cardboard carton
bent out of shape and bleaching among the weeds.
But there were no trees, no gate that once opened
for us when we were led out into the world. No sign
of streams, just a mud-cracked ditch and the peeling
stucco on the house planted alongside the lot.

Isaac

("What is there left that I can do for you, my son?"
Genesis 27:37)

I did not see that I was bound to the stone
of my grief. I spent my childhood playing games—
nothing out of the ordinary. How could such heartache
happen to me? Nothing prepared me. Then, without
knowing it, I wanted exemption from life.
Marriage might come riding in some day,
but the main thing was my life remain the same.
Come to me; I will hold your head in my lap,
give you my last blessing—the blessing that gives
nothing but itself. Never mind Jacob; come to me
so I can hug you. We're closer than ever before;
for you it was your mother, for me my father—
those abettors of countless grains of sand,
those promoters of numberless stars in the sky.
Someone's always paying the price for the promised
land, the new order, the greater co-prosperity sphere—
whatever they're calling it nowadays. Come
to me and I will tell you how my hurt churned
in me, a hidden current, even as I raised sheep,
surveyed lands, entertained kings. And as you listen
you will see how you, like me, played your part.
(I myself think of my quietness and my passivities.)
Then you will possess your life and break the grip
your brother has on you. And one day, perhaps,
when you hear he's nearby, you will go out
to meet him—openhearted—your vexation
and regret gone.

I imagine deliverance
is like that. By telling you all this I go down
to my own Egypt and return.

Poem Without a Name

(after Avrom Sutzkever)

I drift to a gray region, and I'm pulled
downward to the dream-entrance. Under
my sleep I awake in the Bronx Zoo. The exits
clang shut, the slams of lock-up time
in prison movies. Walkways are deserted, kiosks
shuttered, the keeper gone with his keys.

A hand with stars on its fingers moves among
the branches and writes a large R and a large F
above the cages. All their doors fling open
and the animals rush out. They pass the low
barriers and move around me. I am the one
who is trapped now, who is gaped at.

With a hairy soul and a chest smooth and black
as a bed of coal, a gorilla hulks up and asks,
"Why are you trembling so? I'm also two-footed,
and I have a heart like yours. Look, we're not
so different. I only want to feed on your death.
I only want to feast on what we have in common."

A field marshal wearing a monocle while his fingers
are tapping on a map, his swagger stick behind
his back—that's what the leopard looks like
as he strokes me with his paws. He reminds me,
"We once met at a waterhole in Zimbabwe, when you
were on safari. Now I've come to taste your poetry."

Like a young woman with a knowing look, pert
and sleek—as if she were accompanying the coffin
of a parent—a cobra clothed in black hisses in my ear,
"We're both poison. Two doses of poison can poison

loneliness." A yellow-gray slime, shining like
a lubricant, exudes from her crazed skin.

The hand with the stars on its fingers grows fainter,
snake, leopard and gorilla back in their cages.
Keys turn, their bits hidden in the locks. Waking,
in a stupor, I'm haunted by the closeups—charcoal
nipple rising amid an areola of stars, spirals
of sloughs, brown rosettes pulsing on a tawny pelt.

The State of Haryana

A Sikh unwinds his white turban,
shakes out his black hair,
washes it, dries it in the sun,
and waits.

Here in Kurukshetra, in this dust,
in this heat, in this season,
in this daze of light,
not even the station master
knows if my train will arrive.

Wheat glows in the fields.
The rails gleam and disappear.

Coming into the World (1961-3)

We climbed the rusting coupe beached at Fajardo and stood
on the roof, facing the Atlantic, you seven months pregnant.
Our toes gripping our zori, I led you down past the jagged
edges of the split windshield, onto the hood, to the tricky hump
of the fender, and then the awkward stretch to the blistered chrome
on the bumper, where you wavered, before the long step to the sand.

Fallen palm leaves bleached on the shore like serrated flounder
abandoned by the tide. When the cutting season began
the rats came out from the canefields and invaded the backyards
of Country Club, where each man sat under his red banana tree.
When we visited Haiti, each night we heard rats scratching
behind the walls. Our own island tense, the missile crisis blew over.

The birds of paradise were in flight among the bougainvillea
and the flamboyant with their drooping trumpets of dark orange.
That night and that morning when you were coming into the world,
my child, I looked at large vascular leaves and studied
the low clouds over Rio Piedras. I wasn't far away, but out
of sight, staring out the window of the waiting room.

The Photograph of Yankev Glatshteyn Near My Desk

He rests in a rocking chair, eyes closed.
Sculpted in clay, his bust perches on a bookcase.
His wife is at her easel, the curtain
across the window a gauze of light.
Does his sleep inspire her?
Does silence convey forms between them?

The Buddha Glatshteyn is deep into himself.
He is in the region where poems breed,
his head under his head, his hairy arms
circling into the clasp of his hands, as if he holds
his own sleep in his lap. His legs crossed,
a thigh rises from the crease of his groin,
the knee capped by a chevroned light.

Poet—I now can read your language,
language that began to murmur,
to caress me, in my middle age, for
only then could I see what was engrained in me,
the textures, the impressed and the raised.
As you sit there with your eyes closed
I enter you. I descend with you. I reside
in the Yiddish words within you. I accompany you
back to Lublin, to the streets you walked as a child.

Now, you visit me, descend
with me, back to Brooklyn,
help me understand wrong turns I took,
the chances I refused. Be at my side as I walk back
into mailboxed foyers, hallways where the stews
and roastings filled the pores of the air, homes
where upholsteries fitted inhabitants to their rooms.
Guide me and show me how a poet can be

as hard as stone, can look without flinching,
can see the channels he has drilled from his own life.

Speak to me in Yiddish, slowly,
so I can follow you, grasp the nuances, live
in those sounds I once despised and left behind.
In your own words, confront me with all
I wanted to avoid—the cracks, the ash,
the saltant red flecks, the unhinged sky.
Accompany me, as I descend into parts of myself
I once betrayed, disguised, misnamed.
Be at my side when I reappear
at stoops, doorways, stairs with their faded runners.
And as you gesture and speak to me in Yiddish
I will understand. We will converse and sit
among those scenes I once shunned,
and you will smile, delighted at how scorned
and base Yiddish quickens in the haunts where we talk.
Then you will return to your room, to your nap
under the sculpted head, and I to my life.

Specimen Days

A scoured luster appears on the stainless-steel pitcher,
like scratches from a Brillo pad suddenly caught by the light.
Half naked, shivering, I clutch the handle, a wedge-shaped seven,
and guide my stop-and-go flow with my other hand. The crown
of my penis, smeared iodine-brown, pokes over the cold lip.
A purplish-red blob, like sea-floor vegetation, sways under
my pink urine. When the doctor inserted his tube and took a look,
Marilyn, the nurse, wearing a long blonde ponytail, tossed away
her patch of gauze, held my hand, and comforted me. Later,
I remember how I held the tiny hands of my grandson as the *moyl* snipped
off his foreskin and a glistening purple dome emerged from the nub
of his sex. The *moyl* stanched the blood and hid the piece of skin
between two ribbed cotton pads he placed in a Glad-lock plastic bag,
the size of a change purse. He sealed it between two fingers
and then cradled the baby. "Say hello, say hello," he urged him.
The edge of his finger rubbed wine on the new gums. That night,
under the mobile, my grandson slept with a hand in his crotch.

Steve, the ultrasound man, reassures me as I turn on my side.
He pats the ridge of my right buttock. My doctor and a woman intern
I never see, though I feel her hand and hear her voice, tinged
with an accent I can't quite place, reach inside me and chat
on the cause of induration. "It's a large one," he says.
And now they prepare to draw the truth out of me. Though lubricated,
I flinch and groan as Steve thrusts in the tube. He assures me
that's the worst. The doctor names the coordinates on the monitor,
jokingly charges Steve with taking centimeter liberties. Aiming
the needle, Steve says, "I see exactly the spot I have to reach."
Each time, I hear a click in the machinery before the core is touched.
I'm only my insides as I'm open to every move they make. Far
into his maneuvers, the tissue taken, Steve pats me on the ridge
of my buttock again, says, "I'm almost through," and eases out of me.
He kindly wipes me clean. I climb down from the exam-table,

wobble. He holds my elbow and shows me my prostate on the monitor.
It looks like a rock. He clicks off the screen while I pull up my pants.

Waiting for results, I walk around Mount Auburn Cemetery, drawn,
once again, to Yankee names past their peak—Dana, Lowell, Shaw,
Steadman—black spears fencing some of the plots. The outer reaches
of the grounds shine with the new stones of Simienko, Avedesian,
Malamud. Limbs are still scattered and trees downed from the surprising
storm last spring. I go down the dirt path to the pond. It looks
like a stage at the bottom of an operating theater, yet sacred—
enclosed and secluded with its bent of trees, hanging moss,
cloisters of foliage. On the pond the scum of algae looks
so thick you'd think someone could walk on it. I throw in a stone.
It plops, sinks, and a small circle of water opens up, holds briefly,
and then the green scum creeps back and covers the momentary opening,
like a shutter on a lens, infolding, closing out a scene.
"Learn to offer all you've withheld," I tell myself, as I see
the green-stained vaults, like dormers, protrude from the slopes.
I turn and climb the path toward the gate, up from the pond
shrouded in green, wondering if it's not too late to move
through those protective camps I set in front of me, like Jacob
marshaling all that he owned between himself and Esau,
only to find that nothing saved him except weeping on the neck of his
brother.

a.m.

The sun's confined, the room a morning-dusk, but past my ache
I squint at the blinds and slowly come to see louvered light
mounting like yellow rungs on the upholstered chair. I make
out a clay flowerpot standing on the stained bookcase
flush with the sill. Stems and leaves of tulips rise
in high relief against the overlapping white slats, the jagged
cups of red like crowns from a child's birthday party.
Thin bands ring in the pale white curtains at the frame,
their swell and fall like drapes at the sides of a stage.
Then I remember it was my friend who brought the flowers
and told me (after I assured him I hadn't heard the story before)
how he ran away from Buchenwald after liberation, wandering
the woods for a day, smelling wild flowers and looking for deer.
An American patrol found him, and he told them over and over
about the flowers and the fawns and the does—their heads,
their spots, their eyes, and the ways they leaped. Like a coping
saw, his hands carved in front of their eyes the antlers
of the elk that had stood in the clearing. How strange,
he said, he must have appeared, excited, his neck forward,
his striped sleeves flapping, his speech rushing against their ears.
They winked at each other, then hitched up their rifles again,
their thumbs hooked under the grainy slings, and left him sitting
on the ground, humming Romanian songs at the trunk of a tree.

For Rabbi Ben-Zion Gold

Tendons ridged as your hand raked the page,
the fine pink and white striations of your nails
channeling light. Half-moons emerged from cuticles
and the yellow-white tips out-edged the fingers.
Finally, you found the name of Moyshe Friedman,
the Boyaner *rebbeh*, and your index finger tapped
on his picture set among the Yiddish words. A boy,
you saw him in the flesh in '36, when he visited Radom—
his royal carriage, entourage, the long silk caftan,
the sash, the round hat trimmed with red fox fur.
"I never saw anyone with a presence like his."
You read aloud the passage about him at Auschwitz,
separated from his followers. Like the others who
had just arrived on the *transport*, he took off all
his clothes. Then he walked up to the *Obersturmführer*,
gripped his lapels, and told him in vigorous German
his people would pay for this blood. Jews would continue
to live. He returned to the others, found a hat,
and recited the *Sh'ema*. The other naked Jews repeated
the prayer. Then I remembered you told me that once
while you were digging a ditch in Belsen, a guard
grumbled, "God it's cold," and you told him,
"God will punish you and your people for what
you're doing."
"He could've killed me on the spot."

I have bitten my nails all my life, often down to the quick.
But suddenly, as I was hearing you read and watching
your fingers, I wanted my nails to grow like yours.
In the lamplight, they glowed like amber horns.

New Poems

I

On the Ground

Sitting at my side and wearing
my Basque shirt of childhood, its
bands of red and white taking
turns from neck to groin, you shake
your parti-colored sieve and watch
the strained dirt build up to a peak.
How much I have relied on you
to guess at things, to know
what to reach for and bring
to the light. It's high time
we both moved on, yet we're still
part of the same green act,
you the seed coat
out of which the leaves come.

Playbill

Just the two of us on stage,
an old girlfriend and me performing
a modern dance at the City Center.
At the same time I was watching, sitting
high up and way back in that Islamic barn,
where the last balcony edged
on a catwalk. Dust glittered
in the rays from the canisters
of light perched above me.
In dream-closeups high reliefs
of lunulae and ogees studded the walls.
On stage we kept merging and separating
with our Martha Graham movements—
half Greek tragedy, half barefoot Freud—
stark, bony bodies, a taut skirt,
a fist jammed into a breast. Staggered
panels of paris green made a background
from wing to wing. A white, ovoid
Noguchi stood abstract and dumbfounded
near a bush that arched like a tree.
Chamfers of red velvet gathered at the sides,
and the lip of the stage rimmed the pit.
Muscles tightened and flexed.
Space intoned. We moved into this setting,
hunching, springing, leaping, trying
to mate the music to our bodies,
to reach something splendid in the air
and keep it in the footwork of our landing.
Sometimes so caught up in our movement
we outgrew the angles of our training.
Part of me on stage, part of me
watching from the back seats—no opera
glasses, no schooling in the art,

no terms at my command—
I was ignorant and joyful,
not trying to understand how I could
be dancing, yet far away and looking on.

Walking the Outer Cape

The shine on the littoral lifts off as if it longs
for the backwash that loans it a brief gleam.
The waves wash what they themselves have brought
or bared.
                    I remember Brighton Beach one afternoon
when I was afraid to tell a girl I loved her
as she sat glowing in her bathing suit held up
only by the mold of her body. I did not let that love
wash over me, not worrying about where we would
be thrown.
                    When I was a child at the beach
I let the waves toss me up on the shore, as I risked
the salty taste in my mouth, the abrasive landing, the sand
in my trunks, and let the water do with me what it would
until exhausted and happy I stumbled back to the blanket.

Downward

(“It is impossible to forgive whoever has done us harm,
if that harm has lowered us. We have to think that it
has not lowered us, but has revealed our true level.”
Simone Weil, *Gravity and Grace*)

The receiver pulsing back signals, the postmark
from a place we didn't know a friend had travelled to,
sudden turns too late for directionals—
it always begins with signs we don't want to construe
while we fix the fabric for the heartbreak
that soon will be needled in. Then what we did,
or what we said, leads us back to old scenes
and old lines, to a father's watch and chain,
transformed from a century's curio to the device
of his split-second authority—time keeper whose thumb
clap of the cover over the golden numbers on the face
was the noise of his hand closing a tiny door on the soul.
Agents book memory for a long run in the house
where the child's eyes could not penetrate the iron
bun packed at the back of the grandmother's skull,
where his mother's fists blindly tightened the bow
at the back of the apron, loops as large as a halter.

Yet years later someone comes whom we let in, the memory
set for fresh storaging—red sweater under a gray jumper,
a Schubert cycle at the Y, warm chestnuts
shared on the winding path back of the museum.
All too human the confederation of pleasures, the gambol
of soul-mating. But when the past worms through,
clinging to us during the whole-hearted affair,
and we sink back to the old level of ourselves, defeat
is what we are left with. And so we are bared to ourselves,
like stains exposed on the pillars of a bridge when the water's down,
and staring at a brownish crust or mossy coating on the stone thighs,
we wonder what other shades or vegetation cling below.

The Gulf Sign

The Gulf sign glared
above my summer streets
when I was twelve. A
white oval and blue lettering
cut the orange sun
in two yet conveyed
Louisiana, Texas, Oklahoma,
southern states where oil
gushed through latticed corridors
of derricks and rained down
a glittering darkness on helmets,
drilling rigs, wheels, bores thumping
and thumping into the earth—
the oil drenching everything,
discovery allowing it to spurt
and spurt for the sheer pleasure
roustabouts took just in looking at it,
liquidity of fortune not yet
capped, funneled and barreled.

Last night, my hand stirred light
into the water turning red
from crystals of Jell-O, and I saw
gleaming quivers on the surface
and chance congregations of tiny
bubbles on the mixture's edge.
As I whisked, that Gulf sign
of sixty years ago appeared
in my little whirlpool
in the Pyrex bowl, trying
to meld into the shining red
mixture with its velvety whorls,
fluid ridges and brisk shadings.

Though I knew this pleasure
had to end, I couldn't stop
turning the spoon, I myself
making the swirl of light,
and that sign which so long
lay inside of me blended
with this substance my hand
kept stirring and stirring.

Late Powers

I think of that Richard who sat on a stool in prison
and brooded about who he was and what he did, who fell
from his political rhetoric in the early scenes, from tangled
theories of nature, metaphor and monarchy, into clear
words that told him the truth about himself—the pride,
the insolence, the boasting, the avarice, the rash ambition
that couldn't look itself in the eye, all that disdain—
who came to see himself only when the old might dropped away,
when he had lost pendant, seal, and all the trappings of office.

I want to go down into my own truth yet also move through it
and, unlike that former king, outface the figures that threaten me.
I want to fall from my regrets into possession of myself,
to see, to look into the mirror yet not smash the glass
out of anger, despair, self-reproof, or because I was afraid.
I want to face what made me, then reside outside of my sorrows.
But perhaps regret was given to me as both grief and gift,
that forest of memory with its vines and pools, exposed
roots, delicate hairs, clotted dirt, embedded stones, new shoots.

Ant Nest

Ant nest, forest-underlife,
shattered by my curious poke,
your labyrinths, layer after layer,
fallen into dust—look,
my head falls and cracks open,
teeming with ants—words.

And each word—up, down and over,
from nerve to nerve, through serums
and spheres, then scurrying from crannies
with little white eggs in their mouths.

(translated from the Yiddish of Avrom Sutzkever)

Gather me...

(after Avrom Sutzkever)

Gather me from the ledge of time;
nest in me, like letters from a burning *siddur*.
Gather me together—I will become myself,
alone with you—our bodies entwined.

Find me in a grave, between this world and the next,
wondering which world is better.
Find me set on revenge for a single tear,
cooling my hot knife in the snow.

Think, that cloud darkens with my remains;
it bursts, with my face flashing down below.
Gather me together—I will become myself,
alone with you—our bodies entwined.

To Maya

I admire you just for being here—each atomizer-
sneeze, lubberly kick, or wail at the diaper change.
You breathe onto my chest and into me, as if in holding
you I hold my own soul. Already you have taught
your mother how vulnerable she was just by making
sure you'd arrive. Even before you were born you
were just like us, ready to enter life, yet
at the last minute needing a hand to get you out.

We watch you grow—the nails, the fingers, the changing
whorls of your ears, the wider yawn. We pretend your eyes
follow the mobile as it idly changes shapes above your crib,
or our hand promotes the shift. We hover over you, pleased
in looking, as if we've never looked at anyone so closely.
Some night, when you are older, we will go out and look
for the Pleiades, especially Maia, and I will tell you
how those stars arrived there—how, pursued by Orion,
they were afraid and prayed to the gods, who transformed them
into doves and placed them in the sky, a constellation
telling navigators it was the season to set sail.

I support your head and put the nipple against the back
of your mouth, and Blake's phrase, "sweet babe,"
takes flesh in my hands. An odd mixture of weakness
and pleasure surrounds me. I burp you and hear you belch
and gurgle. My hand on your back feels you breathing
as you lie above my heart and at my shoulder. Upstairs,
your mother's pumping more milk for you, and I vaguely
remind myself of all the things I don't know first hand.

Then my eyes close, just like yours, and we share a sleep.

II

Three

("his eyes shone at her,
Never to leave her face..."
Ovid, *The Metamorphoses*, VI)

I
Philomela

Contagion, baby rashes, prickly
heat came to me when I saw
the red spots his cartridge belt
had scored on my belly. Callused
slaps woke me up whenever I fainted.
I was a trench, the mud of the trench.
He pushed off of me, rose, stood
above me, hitched up his fatigues,
camouflage on the flap
of his fly. He straightened
his helmet and jerked the strap.
The gore of a boot
narrowed, where an olive-
green and mustard leg
went into the leather.
The crack of space
between the corner of his heel
and the ground moved away from me.

I got confused in my testimony.
Threads unravelled.
I've grown wings.

I sing often.

II
Procne

Tereus climbed all over me, his salty
shining skin prowling,
wherever it wanted to go.
Big-bellied, I waited for him
to empty himself and roll away.
Itylus came out red, slimy, bawling.
Then the afterbirth leaked out of me.

Reading Philomela's stitchwork
I thought of Tereus
ripping into her. I saw her
gasping, bleeding, crawling,
her tongue in the dust.
I thought of slicing him up
while he was sleeping.
"But no," I decided,
"this way he'll never lose
the taste of his son."
Now I've had enough of what I did.

But night after night, Itylus
still holds his hands out to me.
Red as a lobster, he tries
to cry "Mother," but he
can't say a word. I'm afraid
to touch him. My mouth is open,
dry. But nothing comes out.

III
Richard

I side with Philomela, her prolonged
stunned grief, Procne wrong in wanting
to put her past behind her. Then
I think of how my work clings
to memory, how it's embedded
in what happened, what I fix on,
what I keep coming back to,
even scenes I've invented.
I think of how my work's like a steep
quarry I drive down to every day, stones
wedged out, lifted, loaded into my truck.
Suddenly, I wonder, who am I to judge
Procne, to insist she remain
gripped by her past—she who's had
too much of memory, too much of grief,
too much of anger, revenge, harm, loss?

For Three Killed by Stalin

I think of Bergelson groveling, pleading at the trial, then shot
    by a firing squad on his sixty-eighth birthday;
of Mandelstam freezing, psychotic, with "paralysis of the heart"
    in the gulag;
of Babel spilling his guts about spying, terrorism, parasitism
    in the interrogation chambers of Lubianka.
I think of them far from their novels, poems and stories, far
    from their faces on the covers of their books;
holding onto another prisoner, who feeds them, helps them walk,
    listens. But maybe none of this happened and they were alone.
I don't want to read about Mirele walking to the outskirts of a
    shtetl; about foreign embassies and gulls shining along
    the Neva; I don't want to read about a boy and the docks
    of Odessa.
I think of Bergelson, Mandelstam and Babel reduced
    to madness, fear and hunger, curled up and mumbling to
    themselves in their bunks.

Then I read them again, forgetting how they died.

Report from the National Commission

("There shall be an end of them here in this wilderness; here they shall die."

Numbers 14:35)

Paper cuffs frilled their chops and they relished
the sluggish sauce in the gravy boats.
They adored statues of gold, jewels chased
into precious metals. They jeered envoys
returning from sacred missions. They ignored God,
who set fire to clouds, suspended the sun,
who forbid them to be zealots of ease. But
they practiced evasions with cunning prayers,
palliative charities, oblations of waxed fruits,
perforated doilies, samplers, amulets, plaques.

We had to learn to step over their bodies, not
to falter, not to take pity, not to look back,
but leave them where they stumbled and collapsed
from the weight of all they carried—household gods,
brocades, salvers, birdcages, crockery, consoles.
Carts crammed with trunks clogged the roads. Wheels
wobbled under the load. The baggage proved too much.
Balking, petty, unappreciative, they spurned
the power that could take them from the wilderness.
When they died out, we could enter the land.

Isaiah and Homer

Leyeles, craftily, your poem honors Homer,
whose gods and mortals interplay. Sun, oxen,
moon imbrue the warriors. A child-like nobility
emerges from their desires. Yet
I can also hear in your poem—"feh, feh"—
all that boasting, heroism, animal gleam
of human bodies, the polymorphic divine—
none of that really for Jews, rather,
Isaiah's exhortations for justice, rhapsodist
of brotherhood—enemy animals sleeping
in the same stall, weapons recycled to farming gear,
everyone praying under one roof. God forgives us again.

Leyeles, why don't you mention the Books
of Joshua and Samuel and Kings? Look at David!
How Homeric he is, warrior who writes poetry
and sings tales. He takes women as prizes of combat,
snips off hundreds of foreskins for the bridal price,
loves a man whose death in battle makes him rip
his clothes, weep, fast, and write a dirge. He faces
incest, factions, betrayal in his own palace.
And think of what you omit about Homer—
Priam kissing the hand of Achilles, that marked
man reminded of his own father; Andromache
worried sick about the future of her son;
those bristles of horsehair cresting the helmets
of doomed heroes; fate versus free will dramatized
in the disguises and interventions of the gods,
in interlocked schemes and passions of the warring sides.
Ah, Leyeles, how much you leave out in order to praise
Homer but choose Isaiah—nothing
in your poem like Chernichovsky's prayer to Apollo,
his heady sense of himself as both Jew and Greek.

Leyeles, it's a masterful poem you've written,
recurrent Yiddish rhymes in praise of Greek heroics,
of the scale and spectrum of their universe; then
you side with the prophet's cry for pity,
each stanza compelled to end with the name Isaiah.
I wish you had broken the link of your rhymes;
they shackled you to a preconceived point of view.
I wish you had pierced the probities of your ideas,
surprising your own upbringing, storming yourself,
racing past your own positions. Or I wish you had
sneaked off by yourself, sulking, stripping yourself
of the armor of your loyalties. Break down your forms,
Leyeles, or let them carry you to your contradictions.

O, Leyeles, let us sound out our souls
together, in Yiddish, like that movement
in the last "Rasoumovsky" quartet where the German
imbues the Russian motif with a Jewish longing.
Leyeles, let us remember how Esther stems from Ishtar,
how she assumed the garb and wiles of the love goddess.
Let us face the music that has made us,
knowing we are not entirely one thing or another,
the old Jew in us opening our tent to the dusty,
hungry strangers who come with procreant news.

Joseph in Egypt

You learned to watch yourself, never revealing
your brothers stripped you and sold you, never telling
anyone the whole affair between you and Potiphar's wife,
never letting anyone know your thoughts when
the warden made you his trusty in the Round Tower.
You learned the ropes of your profession, advancement
taking its course. Yet how often you were stupefied
by your own dreams: Why did the coat spread above you
like a starless sky, or why did the serpent tighten
your golden headband? No one to tell your dreams to,
to help you understand them, though you impressed everyone
with your interpretations of theirs, the connections
you drew between their images and the national fate.
How much of yourself you had to hold back or never understood
as you made your way in Egypt. Now you look back, marvelling
at what drove you down the road of your success—
how you became an expert in storage, a genius in
persuading ruling powers to delay the eating of the harvest.

Now you see all your scheming led to the moment
when you would break down before your brothers—
when title, signet ring, stylish beard, fine linen
and gold chain didn't mean as much as weeping
with your brothers, all of you alone, sitting
and shaking on the floor of the receiving hall,
telling and listening to stories over and over,
filling in the details of childhood and the years
you were apart. You found out about this one's guilt,
that one's dream, still another's failure, the sacks
of grain bulging and leaning against the long wall.
Your foreign murmurings and cries were like a strange music
to your adjutants and clerks, listening behind closed doors.

****

When you and your brothers were lamenting on the threshing
floor at your father's death, as if you were still trying
to allay the old resentments—the favoritism, the ridicule,
the pedigree, the revenge—the Caananites of Atad
were stunned at how bitterly Egyptians mourn, not knowing
you were Hebrews, a tribe they hadn't seen for decades.

Saul at En-dor

("He inquired of the Lord, but the Lord did
not answer him, whether by dreams, or by
Urim or by prophets."
I Samuel 28:6)

The witch's hands shake so much,
food falls from the plate
she places at my shoulder.
I'd rather eat this dirt. Why
should she, or anyone, be afraid
of me? Frowning on me,
He plays favorites,
uses me as an object
lesson.
So, kill
me off—then cranes latticing
the sky, escalators
rising in glass atriums, crated
goods sunning on the quays.
Grinning below the headline,
the young Sinai commander's
helmeted in a blood-stained bandage.

All right. I'll get up, take something,
and leave for the front with my son.

The Third Elder

("and they were obsessed with lust for her."
Daniel and Susanna, v.8)

I was walking on my roof after lunch,
enjoying my cigar, blowing smoke rings,
watching them widen, shimmer and disappear.
That's how I happened to see her bathing
in her garden. Her nakedness took me by surprise,
white and gleaming, like a ghost in the flesh.
She glanced upward at the leaves. I ducked
and hid behind the sheets on the clothesline
and watched her moving the sponge around
her body, rivulets of soap glistening down
her shoulders and breasts towards her belly,
half in the water, half above the water.
She stood up, stepped onto the grass and reached
for a towel, damp ringlets clinging to the nape
of her neck as she bent towards the earth.
I wished my middle finger could graze her back,
trace her skin as it slopes down from the spinal
ridge and stretches smoothly towards hips and ribs,
then creasing into collops of fat
that curve around and vanish in the midriff. She rubbed
her hips strenuously with the towel. I could feel
the pile bunching under her fingers. Her hand
drifted across her haunch, rubbed circles on an
inner thigh and rose to the delta of hair.
The right foot bent outward, the sole tilting up.
I didn't think I could get an erection anymore simply
by looking. Her arms found their way into the sleeves
of her red striped robe. She made a bow from the dangling
belt and wound a fresh purple towel around her head
like a turban the Queen of Sheba might wear.

O Safath and Tobith, my old cronies on the bench,
I understand why you sneaked into her garden.
When I pass her on the street and look at her
from under my distant gaze, no one catches me,
some retired gentleman doing his errands for the day.

III

To Walt Whitman

That old man—tramping down Flatbush Avenue—
with a cane, white beard, light brown tunic
and gray felt trooper hat—that was you—
Walt—just like your picture—when you held court
in Camden—avuncular, garrulous and ruddy—
I was climbing up the avenue—where it runs
between the zoo and the botanical gardens—
one of those "ample hills of Brooklyn"—
Why didn't I follow you? Why didn't I stop
and go back down with you? Something kept me in check
as I hiked toward the library—to finish my thesis
on you—You came to turn me around—there
you were—within a foot of me—here on the streets
we shared—and I missed what you showed me—You knew
that would happen—and encouraged me to look
for you again—that's what your beard proposed—I resisted
your very words I memorized—But missing you there—
I took the long way around to find you again—
In '91—when I quit teaching—never to do a seminar
on you again—I ran to the barber shop to get rid
of my beard—which I hid behind since '67—
Sitting on the big chair before the long mirror—
I saw my father's face—I came out from under my beard—

How do we change—Walt? Do you think poetry
has anything to do with it? Do you think we miss
our chance—the way I walked past you—until we
just get tired of the way we are—slowly ready
ourselves—and when that old man—I mean you—
comes back—find that we follow him? Say, the way you
went south—stopped writing editorials—visited the sick
in the city hospitals—owned up to those affections
churning in you—let out your fears of flesh-betrayals—

found your parallelisms and your lists and possessed your world—

I think of our lives—Walt—and they work something like this—
At Castle Garden—where you heard Jenny Lind sing—
and where my grandparents came through as immigrants—
I saw fishes in the tanks—sea horses with their plated
bodies—their beady eyes and crocodile snouts—standing
up in the sand—like curved musical notes—Tentacles
swayed around the mouths of anemones—and the tails
of fishes flicked as they disappeared in the caves—
I saw all this as a child—holding my father's hand—
We are connected—Walt—through that renovated round
building at the Battery—where I feared the glass
would break and all that sea life—and all that water—
come pouring out—drowning me—the fishes swimming
over me—out into the Upper Bay—through the Narrows—
beyond the mouth of the Hudson—deep into the Atlantic—

I think of our lives—Walt—and they work something like this—
I carried you around in my hip pocket—that old
Boni edition—the forest green cover—leathery—
fitting snugly against my ass—I opened you up
on trolley cars buses ferries the el the subway—
Going to work—traveling to relatives—riding around
to escape my bedroom—I read about naked swimmers—
ants on stalks—splotches of moss and lichen—corpses
in the grass—oceans and pavements that spoke to you—
and that spoke to me the same—as if we were one ear—
I read you in my throat as the train made contact
with the third rail—the trolley with the overhead wire—
as the ferry with the accordion gate steamed to Hoboken—
O Walt—I convinced myself I absorbed you—that motion—
that parturient waiting—that sympathy—that listening
to bird, wave, and the grinder sharpening the knife—
But it took me years and years to get to my poem—
borrowing from you—where I recall I never kissed

my father—Even today when I walk the esplanade
at Brooklyn Heights I think of you and Hart Crane
and Melville—making up a past New York
that dwells in me—Once in '55—during my lunch hour—
not far from the place where Lafayette kissed you
when you were a child—I searched out the corner of Fulton
and Cranberry—and there I saw the plaque on the wall—
above two garbage cans marking the place—so it's said—
where you the journeyman set print for what you finally
called *Leaves of Grass*—book of voyages and retreats—
Back then I did not know that you could teach me
how to write out of my cave of despair—I couldn't see
how you had emerged—from the dark vaults of yourself—
Many times I missed you—though you were inches away—

I think of our lives—Walt—and they work something like this—
One high school summer I cut and stacked steel piping—
and kept the green bins filled with screws—at Manny's
Hardware off the Bowery—where you went to the theater—
I walked under the el during my lunch hour and saw
how the fractured light linked with its own shadows—
how rails and ties and girders transformed the streets
to a chiaroscuro that spread to hoods and roofs of cars—
to the drunks wavering on the curbs—to the signs and pillars
of lights—to the green roofs over the subway steps—
Squares of pavements oddly glared in front of the dark
vestibule of a store—or where old-timers huddled at an entrance—
You—Walt—and Reginald Marsh and Berenice Abbott and Hopper
encouraged me to trust my hunch—that what I saw
in the colors and lines and angles of the streets—
in the arms of taxi meters—in the valleys of fedoras—
in the toe cleavages peeping from black pumps—in the lead
clamps that secured plates of glass where they met
at the edges—were recesses of myself—alphabets
to read—fractions of the streets and the shops
lodged in me—Mannahatta-tokens of myself—

Walt—it never dawned on me to walk east
and visit what was left of that Jewish world—
for it took me three decades more to walk *those* streets—
looking for the ghosts of Yiddish writers—entering
the remnants and renovations of their old haunts—
trying to imagine them there—Yet back in '47—
when they were still in the flesh—I walked the other way—
So much so near—I never knew how to grasp—Your book—
Walt—I held it too close to me—and didn't even see
you warned against that—how that too was a trap—

I think of our lives—Walt—and they work something like this—
After the aquarium moved from the Battery
to Coney Island—where you raced up and down
on the sand—and declaimed Homer to the surf
and the seagulls—my kids and I looked at the brown
sheen on the seals—and the suckers on the tentacles
of the octopus—A few blocks away my mother-in-law
was dying—depressed angry her life a waste—she said—
Refusing all help at the end—sliding back—
mumbling names no one—not even her husband—recognized—
she—and her world—went under—never to surface again—
Yet decades later my daughter named her daughter after
that old woman—and at the naming ceremony I read my poem
for my granddaughter—wondering what it's like to breast-feed
a child—even as I hit seventy and brood and nurse my back—

I think of our lives—Walt—and they work something like this

Kafka's Ear

"Two *Tkhines*"—*Tkhines* (plural of *tkhina*) were very popular non-canonical Yiddish prayers in prose for women in Eastern Europe. These poems are imitations of them.

"To the Memory of a Jewish-American Poet Whose Work Came to Too Little"—*goyishe mishigas* (Yiddish)—Gentile craziness.

At the Turkish Bath

"At the Turkish Bath"—*shvitzed* is an anglicized version of the Yiddish verb to sweat or perspire.
—Kaddish is the Jewish mourner's prayer, but is also an affectionate way of referring to one's male heir since the son would honor the father's memory by saying Kaddish for him.

"Yankev Glatshteyn Visits Me in the Coffee Shop"—*zay gezunt* (Yiddish) means be well.

"In Memory of Rabbi Herman Pollack"—*mamzer* (Yiddish) means bastard.

Ice Like Morsels

"For Rabbi Ben-Zion Gold"—*rebbeh* is the respectful and affectionate title of the leader of a Hasidic sect, often preceded by the name of the town in Eastern Europe where the group was centered.

Sh'ema is the central prayer of Judaism, which all Jews know.

New Poems

"Gather me..."—*siddur* is the daily prayer book of Jews.

"Isaiah and Homer"—Saul Chernichovsky was a modern Hebrew poet, who wrote the poem "Before the Statue of Apollo."

Photo by Todd Miller

RICHARD FEIN's poetry, translations, articles, and reviews have appeared in many journals. His books include the poetry collections *Ice Like Morsels* and *To Move into the House;* a critical study, *Robert Lowell;* and a memoir, *the Dance of Leah.* He lives in Cambridge, Massachusetts.